The
ZOO
in the town

Discover the animals which
live in your town

David Taylor & Mike Birkhead

Introduction

The animal and plant life that exists even in the most polluted concrete jungle of a city is still amazingly varied. Much of it is difficult to spot or taken for granted. You may expect to find some living things in overgrown graveyards or round broken-down buildings or abandoned docks, but everywhere, if you have eyes and interest and enthusiasm for nature, creatures and plants are hanging on. Birds of prey visit office blocks in the centre of the city, rare bats find homes in the steeples of city churches, and centrally heated town houses are just bliss for lots of tiny creepy-crawlies.

This book takes a look at just 10 of these townies – animals you will all be familiar with, but may know little about.

First published in Great Britain in 1987
by Boxtree Limited

Text copyright © 1987 by David Taylor
Photographs copyright © 1987 by Mike Birkhead

ISBN 1 85283 003 4

Edited by Graham Eyre
Designed by Grahame Dudley
Typeset by Servis Filmsetting Limited, Manchester
Printed in Italy by New Interlitho S.p.A. - Milan

for Boxtree Limited, 25, Floral Street,
London WC2E 9DS

Contents

Abbreviations

mm millimetre
cm centimetre
m   metre
km kilometre
ha hectare
gm gram
kg kilogram

The Rat

Although some scientists believe there were no rats in Britain before the Middle Ages, and that they arrived on the ships of soldiers returning from the Crusades in the Holy Land (what is now Israel), they probably lived in Britain long before that. These first British rats were *black rats*, which came from the Far East and whose relatives still live there. They often live in the roofs of people's houses, for they

The black rat, a clever climber

are good at climbing.

Black rats took a liking to travelling by ship and in the days of the early Spanish and Portuguese explorers were often eaten by sailors when other food had run out. On one voyage made by an English merchant ship, nearly the whole crew fell ill with the dreaded scurvy, caused by not eating fresh food. One man, however, remained fit and healthy. When asked how he had managed this, he said that he had eaten raw, freshly killed black rats!

The black rat was certainly in Britain by the thirteenth century, when it spread the disease known as the Black Death – or, rather, the rat carried the flea whose bite passed on the germ that caused the disease! The black rat is now rare in most parts of Britain, having been pushed out by the *brown rat*, which arrived around the year 1720, probably

from China or Central Asia. Brown rats are bigger, stronger and more aggressive than black rats, and they got rid of them by eating them and their food-supply. Brown rats don't like any competition, even from mice; where there are brown rats you will rarely find mice. People used to believe that the brown rat first came to Britain on board the same ship as George of Hanover, who became King George I, and for this reason they called the animal the 'Hanoverian rat'. Another theory was that the rat came to Britain hidden among the timber on Norwegian ships. That is why the Latin name of the brown rat is *Rattus norvegicus*, meaning 'Norwegian rat'. It is estimated that in the United States there are 200 million black and brown rats, and that they cost the country £1000 million a year (£5 for every rat) in spoiled crops. One report said that rat hairs had been found in nearly a third of samples of various tinned food products.

Because they have hair and feed their young on milk, rats are true mammals, but they are also rodents. 'Rodent' comes from the Latin word meaning 'to gnaw', and all rodents have one pair of upper gnawing teeth (unlike rabbits, which have two pairs and are not rodents, being more closely related to hoofed animals such as cattle and deer). Over 40 per cent of all mammal species on earth today are rodents. There are

The brown rat

The rat, a typical rodent

dozens of different species of wild rat in the world.

What is the difference between a rat and a mouse? It is not just a matter of size, for there are small species of rat and large species of mouse! To scientists, 'rats' and 'mice' are simply names given to various species within the animal family called *Muridae*. Rats have more rows of scales on their tails than mice have. Rats have 210 or more, but mice never have more than 180.

Apart from the brown rat and the black rat, there are *water rats*, with large flattened tails that they use to swim with, *swamp rats, tree rats, field rats, jerboa rats, bamboo rats* and *kangaroo rats*, to name but a few. Jerboa rats have long hind limbs and tufted tails and are found in north Australia. Africa has giant rats 75 cm long. In the Solomon Islands in the Pacific you will find a woolly rat, while New Guinea is the home of *Mallomys*, a very large species with gorgeous long hair

speckled with white. *Anisomys* is another rat that lives in New Guinea. It is creamy-coloured all over except for a dark base to its tail. The rarest rodent in the world is probably *Swarth's rice rat*. Only 4 have ever been seen alive (in 1906), and that was the last anyone knew of this creature until 1966, when the skull of one that had recently died was found. The home of this creature (if it is not yet extinct) is on James Island in the Galapagos Islands, off South America.

Disease-carrying wild rats should not be confused with the tame rats kept as pets, which are clean and gentle creatures. They are lively, easily handled and cheap to feed. White rats especially are very common as pets, but there are many other colours to choose from. An acceptable rat should be very much of a busybody, always on the go and rather nosey. It should look clean and healthy, having sleek fur with no thin or bald spots, and it should not mind being handled. The tail must be smooth-skinned and completely undamaged, and there must be no sign of lameness when the rat moves about. If you wish to buy a tame rat, go to a good pet shop or look through the magazines in which rat-breeders advertise. In this way you should be sure of obtaining a good animal.

Rats are very successful creatures. They are tough, breed rapidly and are very adaptable, which is why they can be found in nearly all parts of the world. In the wild, rats generally do not live very long – usually only a few weeks or months. Tame rats tend to live much longer – up to $3\frac{1}{2}$ and sometimes even $5\frac{1}{2}$ years. Rats are alert, with well-developed senses of sight, hearing and smell. They communicate with each other mainly through smells produced by their scent glands and through the various sounds they make. They have in-built homing-instincts but are almost certainly colour-blind, seeing the world only in black and white.

Jack Black, the royal rat-catcher, in his official uniform

Like most small rodents, rats drink very little water; this is because their bodies obtain almost all the water they need from the food they eat. The bodies of larger animals, including humans, also obtain some of the water they need from their food, but they need far more water than rats and so drink a lot too. If you keep rats as pets, though, you must make sure that they always have fresh clean water, because tame rats may not be as hardy as their wild cousins.

Some species, such as the kangaroo rats, are very good at jumping. They have specially sensitive ears, which control balance as well as hearing (to be good at jumping you need a very good sense of balance, so that you don't fall over). Kangaroo rats live in the desert, where it is very useful to be able to hear well too. South American fish-eating rats and water rats are first-class swimmers. Some rats, such as the wild black rat, are very good at climbing. The black rat developed from tree rats, and can dash along telephone wires better than any tightrope-walker. The brown rat can climb too, though many people think it can't; but it is not as clever at it as the black rat is.

Rats can eat 10 per cent of their body weight in food every day, but spoil a much larger amount when they are active in food-stores. 100 rats eat around a ton of cereal grain in a year. In other countries rats damage crops of sugar cane, rice and oil palm. It's little wonder that man thinks of wild rats as a serious enemy and does all he can to get rid of them. He uses all sorts of poisoned baits to kill rats, but often rats quickly become immune to the poison or learn to avoid the bait.

An extraordinary character called Jack Black was Royal Rat-catcher to Queen Victoria. He advertised himself as 'Rat and mole destroyer to Her

Majesty'. His official uniform was made up of white leather breeches (trousers that only reach to the knee), a green coat, a scarlet waistcoat, a gold-banded hat and a belt across the shoulder onto which were fixed four rats made of pewter. Not only did Mr Black catch and kill rats and other pests, but he also bred and sold pet rats, especially 'pied' or 'variegated' rats (rats with patches or blotches of different colours). Some were fawn and white, some black and white, some red and white, some black, white and red, and so on. All these rats were bred from the brown and white rats. Mr Black sold many of his pet rats to ladies, who kept them in cages designed for squirrels.

Rats have not always been thought to be bad things. In olden days many people thought they had magical powers, knowing about the future and able to warn people of danger and disaster. It was also claimed that rats would react to certain kinds of music and magical charms. The famous Pied Piper of Hamelin is said to have emptied the town of Hamelin in Germany first of its rats and then of its children in the year 1284. (There is a poem about him by Robert Browning.) If you go to Hamelin today you can still see the story told in marvellous model figures that appear from behind a clock every hour.

In 1953 a British magazine stated that there was still a rat-charmer working in Cornwall – a man who could attract rats by whistling. The animals would come running to him, and he was then able to pick them up and dispose of them.

The Pied Piper of Hamelin

The Fox

It is always a thrill when I am driving along at night and my car headlights pick out the sleek red-brown shape of the fox slipping into a hedge or through a garden gate. It's a common sight at night in our towns nowadays – often in roads far from the open country. Reynard the fox is becoming, much to my delight, a town-dweller. One thing for sure is that he is safe from the huntsman when he's roaming the town! And what a wonderful creature this master of cunning, this handsome member of the dog family, is. Intelligent and clever, he has long been known for his cunning: in the Bible, for example, Jesus likens King Herod to a wily old fox.

There are 21 different species of fox. Our friend the *red fox*, the only type of fox to be seen in Britain outside zoos, is also the most widespread and adaptable of all the dog-type animals. It can be found from the Arctic Circle to North Africa, from Asia to Central America.

Other types of fox are found in a much smaller area. They include *Blanford's fox* of Afghanistan and the mountains of Iran in Asia, the *crab-eating fox* of South America and the *pale fox* of North Africa. Some species, such as Blanford's fox and *Colpeo's fox* of the Andean mountains in South America, are endangered species. The rarest foxes are the North American *swift fox* and the *small-eared dog* (really a fox!) of South America.

What is a fox? It is a small member of the dog family that has a pointed muzzle, large ears and a bushy tail or 'brush'. With its muzzle it can smell about 1 million times better than a human can; its large ears give it very sharp hearing; and its tail is used for balance when running and for signalling to other foxes.

Although the *bat-eared fox*, which lives in the African plains, lives mostly

Reynard the fox, member of the dog family

on termites, the rest, including the red fox, will eat all sorts of things: dead sheep, rabbits, rodents, birds, fish, frogs, insects and worms, plus fruit, mushrooms and even rosehips! Sometimes fruit can make up 90 per cent of the diet. Foxes enjoy grapes too: the Song of Solomon in the Bible speaks of 'the little foxes, that spoil the vines'. Foxes also have a habit of storing food by burying it. They do this especially with birds' eggs. When they need this food they rely on their nose rather than their memory to find it. A fox can smell out a bird buried 10 cm deep in the ground when passing 3 m away, and it can smell out eggs buried 5 cm deep if it happens to pass within 50 cm of them. Luckily for them, young rabbits buried in the sand by their mother before she goes off looking for food are almost always missed by a passing fox. This is because they have even less of a scent than eggs have.

Good ears, eyes and nose of a hunter

Some foxes actually live in the town and bring up their families there. Gardens and parks and waste ground offer lots of places where a fox can make a den. Other foxes are 'commuters': like people who travel into

A fox's incredible sense of smell

A fox cub close to a city centre

the city every day from the countryside, they live in the country and only visit the town. These foxes usually come into the town at night, in search of the easy pickings to be had round man's rubbish dumps, dustbins, gardens and back-yards.

The fox in the town is no threat to the pet dogs and cats that it may meet on its travels, but it is sensible to make sure that your rabbit-hutch is strong and that the wire netting on the front isn't broken or loose anywhere. The fox has adapted quickly to life in town: there are lots of places for dens, and the fox has found lots of food that it can happily eat. Most important of all, in the town the fox is safe from hunters, gamekeepers and farmers, and modern farming methods have made it difficult for lots of creatures, including foxes, to find enough food.

A fox's home is its den, which may be an enlarged rabbit-hole, an old badger's sett, a dried-up drain or a space beneath a garden shed in winter. In summer red foxes normally rest above ground where there is plenty of cover (trees, bushes or deep undergrowth). They live alone

except in the mating season, when they form groups of up to 6 foxes: one male or 'dog fox' with a number of females or 'vixens'. All females in any group are relatives. When they have grown up, male cubs move out of the group and can travel away as far as 250 km. Even when part of a group, a fox still tends to hunt alone, over territory that can be as little as 8 ha or as much as 2000 ha. A fox claims a territory for its own by leaving droppings or drops of urine around the border.

Smell is important for foxes as a way of communicating with each other. They have glands at the base of the tail, on the lips and between the toes that produce a sweet, musty smell. Foxes also signal with their bodies (for example, by the way they hold their ears or tail) and make a variety of different sounds. Barks, yowls, screams and whines have their own special meanings.

Foxes are good at digging burrows, though species such as the bat-eared fox, which does a lot of digging to find the termites it lives on, are better at digging than red foxes. Red foxes catch their prey by a sort of jump called a 'mouse jump'. The fore-legs rise high and then fall straight down to trap the victim beneath the paws. The nose comes down on the prey straight afterwards.

Foxes mate in January or early February and one litter of cubs is produced each year, usually in March. The number of cubs in a litter averages about 4. Sometimes 2 or more vixens share a burrow and will suckle one another's cubs. A vixen's milk is richer than the milk that a human mother feeds her baby, with 5 times the protein and about twice the amount of fat. When the cubs are older, the dog fox helps feed the youngsters by bringing home dead prey.

Although foxes do sometimes raid hen-pens and poultry-yards, they are *not* a great pest and certainly not so bad that they need to be hunted. The animals have long been admired for their cleverness and courage by country folk and there are many traditional beliefs associated with them. People believed at one time that witches could turn themselves into foxes, and as late as the end of the last century the inhabitants of Kirtlington in Oxfordshire spoke of a local woman who transformed herself in this way. A fine fox was often seen near her house, and was often hunted, but never caught. Once the hounds were so close behind it that it seemed impossible for it to escape, but the hunted animal made a sudden turn and rushed into the woman's house. When, a few seconds later, the huntsmen followed it, there was nothing to be seen but the 'witch'

sitting quietly by her fireside. Or so the story goes! In Wales it is thought lucky to meet a single fox but unlucky to see several together. In many parts of England it is still thought that foxes get rid of their fleas from time to time by taking a piece of sheep's wool in their mouths and wading with it into a pond or river until only their noses are above water. The fleas, to escape drowning, rush onto the wool and the fox then lets it fall into the water and float away. Some folk say that the fox will use a bunch of dry grass rather than wool.

And do you know what a 'fox's wedding' is? When a sudden shower of rain falls while the sun is still shining, country people say that somewhere a fox is being married.

On patrol near London's Tower Bridge

The Wasp

ate summer and autumn is the time when wasps come to town in search of sweet, ripe fruit. We all recognize the wasp, and most of us have been stung by one. The wasp that we all know is the *common wasp*, but it is only one of about 10,000 known species.

Wasps are stinging insects that, unlike bees, mainly hunt other insects, which they feed to their young. Some are solitary and usually live alone, while others form colonies or social groups. Social-wasp colonies are

A wasp's nest in a roof

biggest. Males have 7 segments to their abdomens and 13 joints in their antennae; females (queen and workers) have 6 segments to their abdomens and 12 joints in their antennae.

Common wasps are about 2 cm long, with the familiar black and yellow markings. They live in colonies in beautifully constructed nests made of paper. The paper is composed of fragments of wood chewed and mixed with wasps' saliva. The nests are usually underground in a burrow left by some small animal such as a mouse, but they may be built in the rafters of a building. I have had one on the outside of my garage, under the eaves (the

The common wasp

founded by a single queen. At the end of the season all members of a nest die except the queen, who, after being fertilized so that she can lay eggs, goes into hibernation. The following spring she founds a new colony. A typical wasps' nest consists of a queen, a large number of female workers (who cannot lay eggs) and a smaller number of males. The 3 forms are very alike in colour and markings, but the queens are much the

A nest beautifully built of paper

pointed part under the roof). Inside the colony there are combs of cells arranged in flat layers – unlike bees' honeycombs, which stand up on end. You don't see many wasps about in spring and early summer, because the worker wasps are busy hunting and killing insects such as aphids (greenfly), flies and sawfly caterpillars to feed to their larvae. The adult wasps feed on a sweet saliva produced by their larvae. Sometimes, if the insects killed are rather big, the wasps cut them up into pieces to make it easier to take them back to the nest. Most of the insects that wasps attack are pests, so they can correctly be understood as friends of mankind.

In late summer and autumn, with no more larvae to feed and so no supplies of larva saliva to feed upon, wasps go looking for fruit, jam and other sweet things, often in our houses. But all except the queen die by the time winter arrives. Sometimes you may see the queen wasp coming indoors around October or early November looking for a place to hibernate. She may well settle in the fold of some hanging curtains.

Other social wasps in Britain include the *hornet*, which can be up to 3 cm long and is the largest British wasp. The hornet is quite rare now that so many old trees where it used to nest have been cut down. The *red wasp* has an orange-red abdomen and nests under old leaves, logs or matted grass. The *cuckoo wasp* is so called because it makes no nest but lays its eggs in the nest of the red wasp. The *German wasp* lives in the ground and can be distinguished from the common wasp by the three black dots on its face. The *tree wasp* nests in roof spaces, gaps in walls and hollow trees.

Most British wasps do not live in colonies but lay their eggs in small

A German wasp, with 3 spots on the head

nests together with a supply of food in the form of a living but paralysed fly, spider or grub. Some lay their eggs in the bodies of living creatures such as caterpillars or even the larvae of other wasps or bees. When an egg hatches, the larva starts eating the other creature from inside, but is clever enough not to kill it straight away, leaving until last the parts that keep it alive. Some species of wasp lay their eggs on greenfly and others, such as the *Ichneumon fly* (actually a wasp), lay them on butterfly caterpillars, with perhaps 100 eggs in each caterpillar. *Mason wasps* make nests in the loose cement of walls and place a paralysed caterpillar next to the egg. *Potter wasps* live on sandy land and actually construct a pot of 'clay' made from grains of sand stuck together with saliva. The pot is fixed to a plant, an egg and a paralysed caterpillar are popped inside, and a lid is sealed into place. A female potter wasp lives only 2 weeks and makes several pots during that time but dies before any of her larvae hatch out.

The larvae of *wood wasps* burrow in trees. Some other wasps listen for these larvae with the 'ears' on each of their 6 feet and also sniff them out with their incredibly sensitive antennae. They then bore a hole in the wood using a special long drill on the end of their abdomens and deposit an egg within the larva's body. One kind of wasp larva lives inside oak leaves and produces the brownish bumps that are called spangle galls. Another species of wasp then comes along and lays its eggs in these galls to feed upon its relative's larvae!

Unlike bees, wasps have unbarbed stings that can be withdrawn to use again. Stings are used to kill or paralyse prey and also as a defence against

A parasitic wasp that preys on other insects

The unbarbed sting of the wasp

enemies. The very large yellow and black *Geting wasp* of Sweden gives an extremely painful sting. The sting of a wasp is a hollow needle that injects a liquid containing a mixture of chemicals, some of which cause swelling and burning and others of which can put an insect to sleep or cause it to have

Wasps spread the alarm – by chemicals

convulsions (uncontrolled jerking movements). Sometimes formic acid, the stuff that ants secrete, is also present.

When disturbed by a possible enemy, wasps squirt out an alarm substance. This hits and marks the enemy's body and the smell spreads out and warns other nearby wasps, making them highly aggressive. This is how a colony of wasps can become quickly roused to anger. Like bees, social wasps use scent as an important means of communication, and can find their way about with great accuracy, thanks to a sort of in-built sun compass. Even when it is cloudy they can tell where the sun is, because they are sensitive to light that we cannot see. Wasps have also got a good memory for landmarks.

There is no need to be frightened by the wasp. Respect this fascinating creature, treat it patiently and let it go about its business and it'll do you no harm. The only time of year when wasps are likely to sting people is at the end of summer, when the colony has no queen and has only a few days to live.

The Cockroach

*L*a Cucaracha, the Spanish name from which we get 'cockroach' sounds quite jolly. Besides being the name of the insect, it is also the name of a Latin-American dance. Certainly the cockroach is one of the oldest types of insect and one of nature's cleverest designs, but there isn't really anything very jolly about this common pest of town and cities.

Cockroaches are flat-bodied insects with long thread-like antennae and shining, leathery body-casings. They are

An unwelcome gathering of cockroaches

active at night. They originally came from the tropics, but they have spread throughout the world by being carried from country to country in ships' cargoes. There are around 3500 known species of cockroach, but only 6 are found in Britain. As these insects come from warm countries, in Britain they make their homes in heated buildings, mines and sometimes rubbish dumps, which become warm and damp as the rubbish rots away. Cockroaches love kitchens, coming out at night when all is quiet to eat scraps of waste food. They will eat an amazing variety of things, including bones, paper, clothes, books, shoes and dead insects. They even eat other cockroaches. Above all they love bread and other starchy foods.

It may be that friendly germs living inside their intestines help them to digest their food. Cockroaches must have water and can survive a long time on water alone. The big problem about cockroaches is that they spoil far more food than they actually eat, and spread diseases on their feet and in their droppings. What is more, they make a horrible smell.

Cockroaches themselves do not suffer much from disease. This is mainly because they coat their bodies with a thin oily film containing an antiseptic chemical, which kills germs. But they do suffer from mites which live on their bodies and tiny worms which live inside them. Surprisingly, cockroaches are quite resistant to nuclear radiation and could be the only form of life to survive a war with nuclear bombs, even though they do fight a lot among themselves!

Their flat bodies are perfect for squeezing into tiny cracks, and with their long legs they can run fast. They can run up walls and across ceilings using claws on their feet if the surface is rough, and sticky pads on the legs and feet if the surface is smooth. Adults, but not young cockroaches (called 'nymphs') can easily climb up glass.

Female cockroaches lay an egg-case that contains 10–16 eggs. The eggs

Cockroaches have long antennae for smelling

Long antenna

Long legs and claws on feet for rough surfaces

Flat body

hatch in 40–45 days, depending on how warm it is, and the babies are not grubs or caterpillars but nymphs, which are tiny cockroaches without wings. After moulting several times, the nymphs become adults. The adult *common cockroach* lives for about a year.

Some cockroaches, such as the common cockroach, have lost the ability to fly. The common cockroach is red-brown to black and up to 2.8 cm long.

Cockroaches have big, complex eyes and their antennae give them a keen sense of smell. They use smell to pass messages. Some tropical species are beautifully coloured and much more handsome than the cockroaches found in Britain. Big tropical cockroaches, which flutter or parachute with their wings rather than flying in the usual way, may have a wingspan of up to 13 cm.

One of the famous lost goldmines of the Americas is called 'the Cockroach'. It was hidden deep in the jungle and the gold was easy to get at, but it was full of cockroaches. Millions of them

The body-plan of the cockroach

swarmed throughout the mine, forming a thick moving carpet on the walls and making such an abominable smell that nobody could stand it. If you are *very* fond of cockroaches and can find the mine again, the gold is yours!

Cockroaches' bodies are coated in antiseptic

The Moth

Like butterflies, moths are insects belonging to the huge *Lepidoptera* family. *Lepidoptera* means 'scale wings', and their wings are indeed covered by rows of tiny little scales arranged in rows and pegged on just like roof-tiles. But moths are less popular than butterflies, mainly because they usually are more active by night than by day. The English poet Shelley refers to 'the desire of the moth for the star' and we know how moths are attracted to bright lights and can easily perish in their fascination for a candle-flame. An old Japanese legend relates how the moths first fell in love with the night-fly. To get rid of the moths, the night-fly cruelly told them to go and fetch fire for her. The blind lovers flew to the first flame to obtain the fire, and few escaped alive.

There are over 80,000 species of *Lepidoptera* and 2000 of them can be found in the British Isles. Moths differ from butterflies in several ways: they are generally duller in colour; they have stubby furry antennae without blobs on the ends; and when they are at rest they usually spread their wings out instead of folding them together, as butterflies do. The life of a moth is similar to that of a butterfly: the eggs are laid on a plant which the caterpillars can eat when they have hatched, and after

The legend of the moth and the night-fly

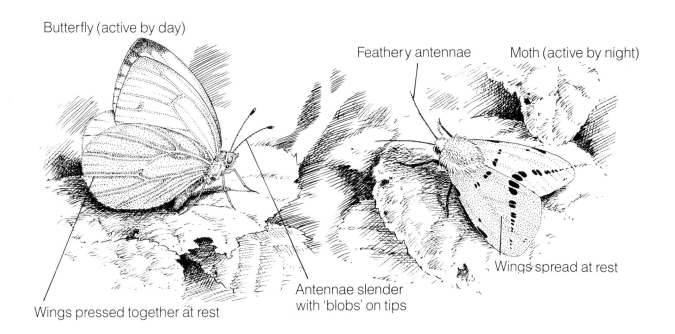

Butterfly (active by day)

Feathery antennae   Moth (active by night)

Wings pressed together at rest

Antennae slender with 'blobs' on tips

Wings spread at rest

several moults the caterpillar stops growing and becomes a pupa or chrysalis. Wrapped up in its cocoon, it slowly changes again and eventually emerges as an adult moth.

Moths have a number of enemies, and one of the deadliest is the bat, a mammal that can fly in the dark and find its prey by using sonar beams – high-pitched sounds that the bat sends out as it flies along and that tell it when there is something in its flight-path. If there is a moth within range, the bat's bleeps bounce off the moth and the echoes return to the bat's highly sensitive ears. From the signal it receives the bat knows just where the moth is. But the moths have developed their own anti-bat night-flying defences! They try to fly silently and have soft furry bodies that soak up sound and send a very weak signal back to the bat. To cut down the noise caused by their wings as they fly through the air, some

Differences between moth and butterfly

night moths have grown a fringe of fine hairs, 2 mm long and 0.007 mm across, that smooth out and silence the movement of the air. Moths also have ways of telling when a bat is approaching. They have special 'ears' on both sides of the thorax, near to the waist. At a range of about 30 m the 'ears' pick up the first bleeps of a bat's sonar. At once the moth changes its flight-path and tries to avoid being picked up by the bat's sonar, for, although the bat is much faster than the moth, it needs to be within about 7 m before it can pick up the echoes of its sonar bleeps and tell where the moth is. To overcome the moth's defences, the bat does not fly in a straight line but reels about in what seems a very clumsy way. In fact the bat is not clumsy at all, and its flying-curves are designed to deceive the moth's anti-sonar. The first

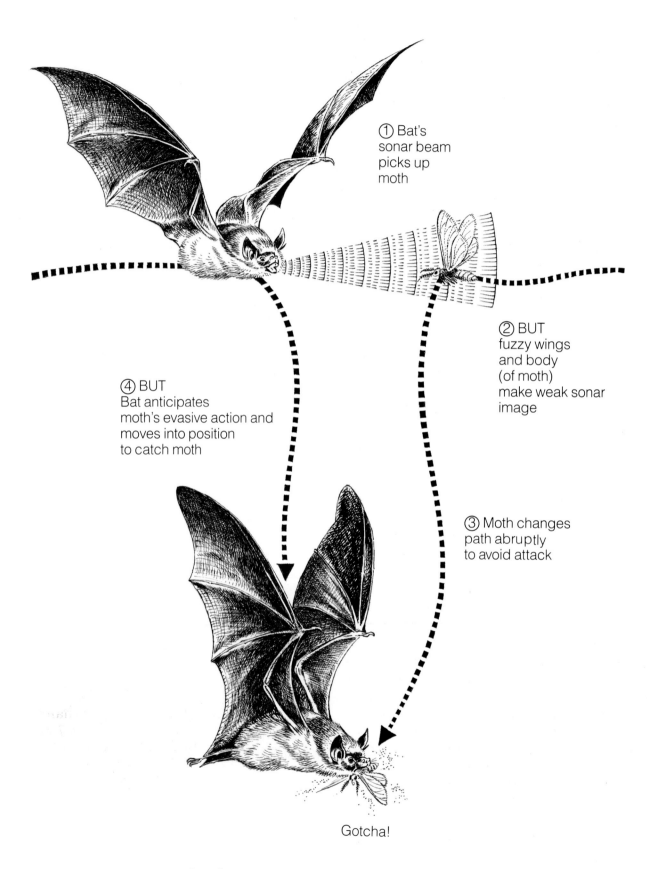

① Bat's sonar beam picks up moth

② BUT fuzzy wings and body (of moth) make weak sonar image

④ BUT Bat anticipates moth's evasive action and moves into position to catch moth

③ Moth changes path abruptly to avoid attack

Gotcha!

A 'dog-fight' between bat and moth

A poplar hawk moth

echoes that a bat receives from a moth when it is within sonar range are about as loud as a fairly quiet car engine!

Once they know a bat is within range, some moths simply fold their wings and drop to the ground, but bats know all about that and have learned to change course so that they can still manage to catch half the moths that try this trick. Many moths are amazing acrobats in the air – looping-the-loop, spiralling and even falling behind the bat and trying to keep there in fights as skilful and tense as one between two fighter planes.

Moths are very good at telling which direction a sound is coming from, but they are completely tone-deaf, unable to tell the difference between high and low notes. Some moths produce sounds as soon as the bat's sonar finds where they are. These very high-pitched insect noises warn the bat that the moth is very smelly or tastes disgusting, so as to put it off the chase. The sound is made by a horny grooved plate on top of a sound-box (which makes the sound carry) where the third pair of legs join the body. Some clever moths make this warning sound when they are not really smelly or bad-tasting at all, and the bats

avoid them in just the same way as they avoid insects that they really would want to spit out.

Moths can find their way by the stars. They have eyes that are very sensitive to starlight and they can see and recognize at least as many stars as man can. Like butterflies, moths have an incredibly sharp sense of smell. Male *silkworm moths*, for example, can smell females from many miles away. To do this they use their antennae, which have lots of tiny branches, and on these branches are an amazing total of 40,000 nerve-cells. These nerve-cells can sense the tiniest amounts of chemical in the air.

The largest moth found in Britain is the *death's-head hawk moth*, a very rare visitor from Africa. Its wings measure up to 13 cm across. The largest known moth is the *great owlet moth* of Central

Scarlet tiger moths at rest

and South America, with an enormous wingspan of up to 36 cm. Compare that to the smallest moth, *Stigmella*, which lives in the Canary Islands and is only 2 mm across with its wings fully stretched!

A moth common in British towns, as well as in damp places in the countryside, is the *poplar hawk moth*, whose wings are various shades of brown with a reddish patch on each of the hind wings, close to the body. This patch can be seen when the insect is disturbed and raises its fore-wings. The caterpillar feeds on the leaves of the poplar, willow and aspen trees.

I think that the prettiest species of moth in Britain is the *elephant hawk moth*. It is common in south and central England and is often seen on June evenings feeding on petunias, soapwort and valerian. This moth is most easily found in places such as rubbish tips and waste ground where rosebay willowherb grows. The female lays her eggs on this plant and the caterpillars feed on it.

A cream-spot tiger moth

Common in town: the cinnabar moth

Moth caterpillars are usually far more beautifully marked than the adult insects. Some have similar colours and patterns to the plant on which they feed, making them difficult to see. Some are brightly coloured as a warning to birds that they taste nasty, or have strange designs or peculiar extra bits designed to frighten off or trick attackers. Some have rows of hairs that can cause rashes when touched. In the United States, *puss moth* caterpillars secrete a poisonous liquid that can make children ill. Even more sinister is the *vampire moth*, which lives in the Far East and bites and sucks blood from water buffaloes, deer and other forest animals. However, none of the British moths is in any way dangerous.If moths come into your house, make them welcome, protect them from naked flames and be gentle when you decide to put them outside.

An elephant hawk moth

The garden tiger caterpillar

The Starling

I share my house with a group of talkative, busy and charming friends. We've been together ever since I moved in, and even as I write I can hear one of them talking outside, while another is working on the garden. We get along very well and I don't make

a fuss about the spots of what looks like purple fruit-juice that they deposit on my white car every day: it's easy enough to clean off. I refer of course to the handsomest of our town birds, the starling. Starlings are the fifth most common visitor to the bird-table and, along with sparrows, arrive to dine in large groups. They often nest under the eaves of the house – always in the same place at the corner above my study. They sing to me from the roof-top, and use the television aerial as a concert platform where they can show off by fluttering their wings while they perform. Their song is a mixture of trills, chuckles and clicks, with occasional sharper calls that seem to say 'cheer, cheer', often followed by more little chuckles. The starling is a very common bird in Britain, and each

A starling outside my study

A starling in summer

winter the birds that live in Britain all the year round are joined by visiting starlings from continental Europe. The starling is a bigger bird than a sparrow but not quite so big as a thrush, and has a summer coat of black that gleams with flashes of blue and green and is dotted with white spots. In the summer the beak is yellow. In winter the coat seems less glossy, the white dots are more obvious and the legs are a darker yellow-brown. Young starlings are a greyish brown.

As a group starlings are one of the

A starling in winter

most successful of all our bird species. Unfortunately they are very bossy birds that push other species, such as woodpeckers, out of their homes. There are 106 species of starling in the world, and some of them are very useful at controlling insect pests. For example, the *wattled starling* and *rose-coloured starling* are great gobblers of destructive locusts in hot countries. The *European starling*, though, sometimes does a lot of damage to crops of young

corn, olives and grapes. In Britain starlings are only a nuisance in the centre of big cities, when they visit them in huge flocks. Lots of money is spent trying to get rid of them, but the starlings keep coming back.

Away from city centres, starlings do a lot of good. They eat lots of insects, including some important pests, and they also help the farmer by perching on the back of grazing cattle or sheep and picking off flies, lice and fleas. As you can tell from its name, the tropical starling called the *ox-pecker* does this useful job for oxen. Some foreign species of starling are very fussy about what they eat. The *Brahminy starling*, for example, collects pollen and nectar using a brush-like tip on the end of its tongue. The starlings of Britain, however, are not fussy at all, and will eat all sorts of things. They like to feed in flocks, particularly in the winter. Their long, straight beaks are very strong and can deal with many different types of food. They especially like poking about in lawns and short grass. This poking-action is very good for lawns, letting them 'breathe' through the tiny holes made by the starlings' beaks.

More and more starlings are living in our towns and cities. They are birds who love to do things together, and flocks of up to 1 million of them have been seen in some city centres. They are noisy and aggressive, but it is a wonderful thing on a winter's evening to see a cloud of them following one of their regular flight-paths to their night roost. They come into cities because it is always warmer there than outside. Among their favourite places are Leicester Square in London and the common in the middle of Boston in the United States. In these places some trees are completely covered with starlings.

Starlings usually fly in straight lines. Every autumn great flocks of them fly

from Scandinavia to spend the winter in northern France, southern England and Ireland. These migrations have been well studied by scientists. They have caught over 1000 of these travellers, put a tiny ring on their legs to say where they were caught and then let them go again so that scientists in other countries who find them can tell where they have come from and study their migration-patterns. In this way scientists have proved that starlings hatched in Scandinavia are born with an in-built map of Europe. They know instinctively which direction to fly in to reach their winter home. Older birds who have migrated before can remember landmarks and in addition know how to find their way by the sun and the stars. They even have a magnetic compass in the form of tiny pieces of iron in their heads! Like the compass used by sailors and explorers, this starling compass can tell where the magnetic North Pole is and so help the traveller know which

Evening in London: coming in to roost

way to go.

When in flight, dense flocks of starlings wheel and turn without any bird bumping into another one. No one knows how they do this. Could it be that they have a sense similar to the bat's sonar, so that they can always change direction before bumping into something? If they have, scientists have not yet found out about it.

Starlings don't only build nests under the eaves of houses. They may nest in a hole in a tree or a cliff or up in an attic. The nest itself is a loose, rather untidy construction of dried grass or straw lined by feathers, and in spring the path outside my study is littered with bits of grass and other rubbish dropped by starlings as they go about building their nest. Eggs are laid in clutches of 4–6, and 2 clutches are laid each year, between April and May. The female incubates the eggs, while the male often goes off to mate with a second female. Some females behave like cuckoos and lay their eggs in the nests of other starlings. Incubation takes 2 weeks, and 3 weeks after a hatching the chicks are ready to fly. The male will help feed the chicks of his first mate, but he usually leaves his second mate to feed her chicks herself.

There is very little difference between town starlings and their cousins who live in the countryside. It is just that, like many sparrows, rats and foxes, a large number of starlings have realized the advantages of town and city life. There is food all the year round, and shelter and warmth in the colder months. Many different kinds of bird live in town, and they brighten up the town for many people who live there.

A starling feeds its young

Home is a tree-hole

The Sparrow

The sparrow is a cheerful, harmless little bird, the commonest in Britain. It can be seen almost everywhere, but most people think it dull or boring and take no notice of it at all. In fact the sparrow is as well-bred and interesting a creature as any bird of paradise or monkey-eating eagle – and has proved far more successful as a species.

Strangely, although sparrows are so harmless, in many European folktales and legends they are said to be wicked. A Russian tale relates how when Jesus was in the Garden of Gethsemane all the other birds tried to stop his enemies from finding him, but the sparrows betrayed him by chirruping loudly around the place where he was. They also were cruel to him when he was on the cross. Because of this, the tale says, sparrows are cursed, and their legs are tied together by invisible bonds so that they can never run but only hop.

Our little friend in winter

Sparrows belong to the family of birds called *Weavers*, of which there are 143 species spread across the world. Most true Weavers live in Africa and are,

Sparrows were said to be no friends of Jesus

unlike the sparrows, often very brightly coloured creatures, mainly yellow and red. Some, such as the *golden-palm weaver* and the *golden bishop*, are very attractive little birds. As you can guess from their name, Weavers make their nests by weaving them. Often the entrances are guarded by tunnels, which can be up to 60 cm long.

Although sparrows are unhappy in cages, they do all like to be close to humans. *House sparrows* rarely nest far away from houses. There are 8 species of sparrow in the world that usually nest in buildings. Some species, such as the *tree sparrow* in Britain and the *yellow-throated sparrow* in other countries, nest in trees, though in Britain tree sparrows will nest in buildings when there are no house sparrows about. *Rock sparrows* and *pale rock sparrows*, which are not found in Britain, nest – of course – in rocks! The *hedge sparrow* or *dunnock*, a shy little bird that lives in hedges, is not really a sparrow at all but a member of a family of dull-coloured birds called *Accentors*.

The commoner of the two British

sparrows and the one that lives in town is the house sparrow. It is the third most common visitor to our bird-tables. It is small and stubby, and its beak is designed for eating seeds. All true sparrows are seed-eaters, though the house sparrow is quite happy with bits of bread and household scraps. House

The hedge sparrow or dunnock

Lunch-time

I sit here when it rains

sparrows love sunflower-seeds. Don't forget to put some out in winter!

House sparrows are bold little birds who are often cheeky enough to throw out house martins and take over their

A refreshing bath – of dust

nests. The male is easily distinguished from the female by his bolder markings and the black 'bib' under his throat. House sparrows fly noisily, making a whirring sound. They usually fly in straight lines, but over longer distances they tend to rise and fall. Sociable and often quarrelsome, they love to be in groups and will roost together in winter, often using their old nests to keep warm. Sometimes on a winter's night a tawny owl will swoop towards a group of roosting sparrows, and catch one in mid-air as the little birds take fright and fluter down to the ground.

Sparrows are not good at singing. The song is simply a lot of chirps and cheeps, repeated over and over again, but they are not the slightest bit embarrassed about it. From the way they sing their hearts out, they seem to think they are nightingales!

Watching sparrows is really fascinating. Take time to watch them scolding, squabbling, competing, searching for food, courting and

Courting sparrows

Male

Female

cleaning themselves up and exercising their wings. If you put a shallow tray about 4 cm deep and 20 cm long and wide in your garden (or dig a pit the same size) and fill it with very fine sand or ashes, you will be able to watch your sparrows having a dust-bath. If you are really lucky, a wren may come along too.

House-sparrow nests are rather untidy. They are made of dried grass, bits of paper and any other material that the birds can find, lined with feathers. It is charming to watch sparrows courting. The males often collect in groups, and compete to attract the females by showing off. They puff out their chests and hop around the females with their wings held low. 2 or 3 clutches of 3–5 white eggs with small brown and grey markings are laid between April and August. The female incubates the eggs for 2 weeks, sometimes with help from the male. The young sparrows are fledged (ready to fly) 2 weeks after hatching.

The courtship of sparrows

Don't turn up your nose at the humble sparrow as you see it picking up crumbs in the street, its feathers dark with dirt or soot. Sparrows are wild birds that have chosen to live among us, and they are as interesting to watch as any rare bird. They are also one of the easiest species to watch, because they are so used to people. The sparrow long ago found that life close to man suited it very well. Because it is not too fussy, it found plenty of food in the town. As a seed-eater, it was quite happy to eat bread, which is made from seeds (the cereal grains from which flour is made are seeds). The town also offered lots of warm, dry places to shelter. Many species could not live in the town because they would not find their special food there or the right sort of places to rear their young. Like the rat and the cockroach, the sparrow did not have these problems, and that is why it was able to fit in so well.

The Pigeon

The second most common bird in towns and cities is the pigeon. In Trafalgar Square in London the flocks of pigeons are a tourist attraction and you can buy food to give them. In other places they are considered to be a pest, and poisons, sticky pastes and electric wires are used to stop them from perching on the roofs and buildings. Often you will see notices telling you not to feed the pigeons, but you can still see them in the streets and shopping-centres of old and new towns, keeping an eye open for little old ladies with bags specially filled with grain or dried crusts, or for any scrap that someone might happen to drop.

Lots of people see pigeons every day of their lives but know next to nothing about the history of this common bird. The pigeon I am talking about is the one scientists call the *feral pigeon*, the species seen mainly in towns. It is not a truly wild species, but comes from pigeons that were bred from the wild *rock dove* as racing and carrier pigeons or simply for show – just as pet rats were bred from wild rats. Carrier pigeons are pigeons that can be trained to fly straight home from wherever they are released, carrying messages rolled up in a small tube attached to the leg.

There are several wild members of the pigeon and dove family that live in Britain. ('Pigeon' and 'dove' are just different names for members of the same family.) The *wood pigeon* lives in the countryside and is famous for its call of 'coo-coo-coo-, coo-coo'. The *stock dove* also likes the country, and the *collared dove* has begun to move into town. It first came to Britain from continental

Trafalgar Square's famous pigeons

A wood pigeon

Europe in 1955, and loves grain. It has spread very quickly.

There are around 300 different species of pigeon in the world. Some are very

The collared dove

rare and some have recently become extinct because of man's thoughtlessness. Pigeons can be found in every part of the world except Antarctica and the Far North, and include such exotic species as the *Victoria crowned pigeon*, the biggest of all. I remember how proud I was when we first bred this gorgeous grey-blue bird at Belle Vue Zoo, Manchester, in the early 1970s.

As a family, pigeons have been very successful and have been involved with human beings for thousands of years. White doves were held sacred in many ancient religions. To the Romans they were love-birds, the special birds of Venus, the goddess of love. The ancient Israelites saw them as symbols of purity, and they remind Christians of the Holy Spirit (the Bible says that, when Jesus was baptized, the Holy Spirit came down on him 'like a dove'). Muslims will not kill doves if they can help it. On the other hand, some superstitions hold that doves are unlucky. Welsh miners used to think that if they saw one flying around a pithead there would be a

disaster in the pit.

Pigeons have done their bit in wartime. When Paris was under siege in 1870 during the Franco-Prussian War, carrier pigeons were used to take messages out of the city. These

a few drops and then throw back their heads to swallow.

Pigeons are very good at flying and can travel thousands of miles. The fastest racing pigeon could fly at a speed of 70 km per hour. Like starlings,

messages took the form of letters reduced in size by special photography so that one pigeon could carry lots of letters at the same time. In the First World War one bird carried important messages through the middle of a raging battle and was awarded a medal! In the Second World War the RAF dropped boxes of carrier pigeons behind enemy lines by parachute, so that they could be used to send messages back to London.

Town pigeons, like the rest of their family, have plump stocky bodies with a small head and bill and short legs. They eat a wide variety of foods and unlike most birds drink by sucking water without raising their heads. Other birds dip their beaks into the water, scoop up

The town pigeon has some interesting relatives

pigeons can find their way by the sun and stars and have an in-built magnetic compass. We also know that they must be able to see the horizon when flying in order to find their way home.

Unlike all other birds except flamingoes and the *male* emperor penguin, pigeons produce *milk* for their young. This milk is produced not in an udder (as in cows and other mammals) but inside the crop, a sort of stomach at the bottom of the throat. The milk is rather thick and contains lots of protein, fats, minerals and vitamins. It is brought up from the crop and the young birds put their bills into the adults' mouth to drink it. Both males and females produce milk.

Like their wild cousins, town pigeons feed on the ground. In winter they depend on the scraps dropped or thrown away by man, or the bits of bread and other food thrown down to them by friendly people. In summer and autumn they also eat seeds. When disturbed, they fly away clapping their wings

The pigeon chick gets milk from its parent's mouth.

Pigeons make loose, untidy nests

are laid between March and September. Both parents incubate the eggs, and the young birds are ready to fly at about 5 weeks of age.

Many town pigeons that you will see are not in the best of health. Some of them limp quite badly. They often have damaged legs and diseased joints, and they may have wire or bits of thread caught round their toes or legs. They

together. This is probably a warning-signal to other pigeons.

Males and females are difficult to tell apart except in the mating-season, when the males put on an amusing but beautiful display of strutting, bowing and puffing out their chests to attract the females. Often pigeons nest together in small colonies. Loose nests of twigs and dried grass or paper are built under eaves or on the sheltered ledges of buildings. 2–4 clutches of 2 white eggs

pick up infectious diseases, including food-poisoning bacteria, and can spread illnesses such as tuberculosis to other birds in farms or zoos when flying over or going in search of food. Nevertheless I must admit that I am still quite fond of these interesting birds, and love to sneak them a crumb or two even when there are notices telling me I mustn't.

The Feral Cat

Do you suffer from ailurophilia? If so, you're in good company. Kings, popes, presidents and prime ministers have had it, and I certainly have it too! No, it isn't a disease but the love of cats. And of course the town is full of cats, cats who are owned by people. Or perhaps I shouldn't say 'owned'. Cats, unlike dogs, are too independent to be owned. Many cats own people. They please themselves what they do, and expect to have their own way.

The feral cat, almost wild

But there is another kind of cat that shares towns with people. This is the *feral cat*, the cat you see alone or in groups in the old railway yard or graveyard, on waste ground or in Fitzroy Square in London. Although some of these creatures may be just stray domestic cats, animals out on the prowl or abandoned by their owners, there is a population of cats that are descended from the tame domestic puss but are returning to being true wild cats. They are far more like real wild cats than the contented Siamese or Persian curled up in front of the fire is. You may not realize it as a battered-looking tom cat slips quietly away from you over a coal-tip, but there goes one of nature's deadliest hunters. Under the skin he is basically the same creature as the tiger, the lion and the leopard, as you will see if you can watch him more closely (not an easy thing to do).

The domestic cat in Europe and America probably started off as a cross between two wild species, *Felis sylvestris* and *Felis lybica*. We can be fairly certain that the first tame cats were tabbies and looked very similar to the true *wild cat*, a species that still manages to survive in lonely Scottish forests.

Feral cats are social animals and like being in groups. Lions are like this, but most other truly wild cats live and hunt alone. Also, most species of wild cat cannot breed with other species, but feral cats do sometimes cross with African and European wild cats and their kittens may be either wild or tame.

Feral cats are built just like a leopard, lean and muscular. They stay in trim without having to do any special exercises, though like other cats they like to have a good stretch and this may help them to keep their bodies ready to fight. The cat has a most elastic body. The backbone is held together by muscles, and this means that the spine can bend and turn much more easily than a human's can. The shoulder joint is designed so that the fore-legs can be turned in almost any direction. All this makes the cat very quick and very nimble, able to spring and pounce and twist and run with incredible ease.

The kitten has 24 teeth. These are replaced by 30 adult teeth, 16 in the upper jaw and 14 in the lower. All cats tend to bite their prey in the neck, killing it by breaking its neck. It is fascinating to note that the distance between the left and right fang teeth of

a cat is the same as the width of the neck-joint of its usual prey. A feral or domestic cat has its fang teeth the right distance apart to break the neck of a mouse, and the tiger's are designed to kill the deer and wild pig. There are special nerves linked to the fang teeth of the cat. These sense in the twinkling of an eye when the points of the teeth are in exactly the right place over the neck-joints of the prey. When the nerves tell the brain that the teeth are in the right place, the brain at once tells the jaw muscles to close.

A cat's eyes work well in the dimmest light. At the back of the eye there is a screen made of crystals that reflects every available speck of light and helps the cat to see things we can't. This crystal screen is what makes a cat's eyes flash in the dark.

The cat has wonderful hearing. We have only 6 muscles in our ears, but the cat has 30, which allows it to turn its ears very quickly and accurately to find where a sound is coming from. A cat can turn its ears far more quickly than

Tiger and cat: basically the same

a dog can. Just watch your own cat's ears when it hears a strange noise under the table!

Cats also have a wonderful sense of smell. Their noses are particularly sensitive to nitrogen, which is given off when food is starting to go bad. This

The feral cat walks his patch

The cat has teeth the right distance apart to break the mouse's neck

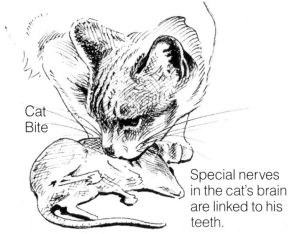

Cat Bite

Special nerves in the cat's brain are linked to his teeth.

The amazing bite of the cat

explains why a cat refuses to eat anything that is slightly 'off'.

We do not fully understand how a cat uses its whiskers, but we know that they have something to do with touch. Removing them can upset a cat for some time. We also know that in the dark a cat's whiskers are amazingly sensitive, helping it to identify things it cannot see.

A ginger Tom at home with friend

A cat has special muscles that allow it to draw in its claws and also to spread them out – for instance, to obtain a better grip. Dogs do not have these muscles, so their claws are always fixed in the same position.

Cats can run at speeds of up to 27 miles per hour, compared with 45 miles per hour for a greyhound and 63 miles per hour for a cheetah. When cats are walking, the front and back legs on the same side move in the same way at the same time. So, for instance, if the front left leg moves forward, the back left leg does too. The only other animals that do this are the camel and the giraffe.

Thanks to their elastic bodies and the extra-fast nerve-link between their ears, brain and muscles, cats can land with their feet down even when falling only a short way. They have also been known to survive very long falls – even from the nineteenth floor of a very tall building (about 60 m). It is extremely cruel, though, to test how far a cat can fall without hurting itself.

Feral cats live in groups. The roughest, toughest tom is 'top cat', and the other cats look up to him as the

Cat Territory

Cats mark out territory by scratching trees and spraying urine.

boss. Every cat knows its place in the group. All cats are territorial, with their own hunting-grounds. Although female feral cats have fairly small territories, they will fight harder to keep them than a tom who controls a large area. The cats mark out their territory by scratching trees, posts and fences, and by spraying urine or rubbing things with a substance secreted by glands on the head and face. Some toms in an area with few cats may control 20 or more hectares. Within its property each cat has its favourite place for sleeping, watching and sunbathing.

Beyond the private territories lie hunting- and meeting-grounds belonging to the whole group. To reach these places cats have a system of pathways that run along the edge of other cats' private territories and areas without cats. Some pathways are the private property of one cat, but most of these paths are 'main roads' that can be used by all. However, there is a 'highway code' for cats using these paths. Any cat approaching a main path from another track must give way to a cat that is

The territories of a cat society

already on the main path.

Cats' meeting-grounds are like clubs where the cats meet at night, groom each other's coats and generally enjoy each other's company. Cats communicate with one another in a variety of ways, including smell, sound and 'body language'. They can produce at least 16 different sounds, and they can signal to each other by the way they move, hold their tails, turn their faces, and so on.

The life of feral cats is often a hard one. People tend to treat feral cats as pests, and sometimes try to poison them, though it is against the law to do this in England. Disease is also common among these cats. Where there are too many cats, attempts have been made to control their numbers by putting out food containing drugs that stop females from having kittens. This at least makes it easier for the other cats to find enough food.

The Bluebottle

When summer comes to town, you are sure to hear the buzz of the bluebottle's wings and the 'plop' as it crashes into a window. People do not like bluebottles in their houses, and no wonder! They are often found in the most unpleasant places and can carry all sorts of diseases. In fact, they are not much better than the house-fly, which can spread over 60 important diseases to

and 6 legs. They possess large compound eyes that can see all around them and antennae that are extremely sensitive to smells. They feed by sucking through a sort of tube called a 'proboscis', which is operated by a pump in the head. As soon as the proboscis touches food (sugar, for example), it will start sucking, and will carry on doing this for a while even if the head is cut off from the body! The

A bluebottle: unpopular insect

people and animals – more than any other creature in the world. The name 'bluebottle' has got nothing to do with bottles, but comes from a Gaelic word (*boiteag*) meaning a maggot. On the other hand, bluebottles really are blue. Another name for them is 'blow-flies'. They are fat and gleaming and come into the house in search of food.

The bluebottle is one of 50,000 different species that belong to the family of 2-winged flies called *Diptera*, which feed on liquids. Like all insects they have a body divided into 3 parts (head, thorax or chest and abdomen)

proboscis contains a set of very tiny teeth which it uses to grate the surface of substances such as sugar so that it can suck them up. (It grates and sucks the food at the same time.) The broad 'lips' at the tip of the proboscis are fringed with hairs that give the fly a sense of taste. The body-surface and legs of the bluebottle are covered in fine hairs which help the antennae pick up the smell of nitrogen in the air. This attracts the insect to dung, meat or dead animals over distances of several kilometres. The antennae are also very sensitive to sounds (only a little less sensitive than the human ear) and help the bluebottle tell which way the wind is blowing, and how strong it is. By this means it can control its speed and flight-path.

The movement of the wings is produced by two groups of very elastic muscles attached to the thorax. When one group of muscles pulls the wing up, the other group is stretched, and the same happens to the sides of the thorax. At a certain point the 'elastic' clicks back and the first group of muscles is stretched while the other group pulls the wings down. This is repeated over and over again. The buzzing noise of the insect's flight comes from the vibration of the thorax as it is tugged to and fro by the flight muscles. The rubbing at the bases of the wings may also have something to do with it.

Bluebottles feed mainly on dung and dead flesh, sucking the juices from them and spreading the germs they pick up through doing this. They lay small clusters of long white eggs on the meat. These eggs are tiny but can be seen quite easily. Depending how warm and

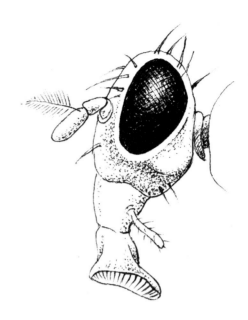

The proboscis is made for sucking liquid

damp it is, the eggs hatch in 12–72 hours and produce tiny larvae or maggots with waxy skins. The maggots' mouth-parts and the casing round the throat are dark and horny and can be seen through the head, which is clear. Inside the throat-casing are tiny cells sensitive

White eggs shaped like tombstones

to light. If there is any light around, they react and tell the maggot to burrow into the meat instead of staying at the surface, where it would dry up and die.

British bluebottle maggots only attack dead flesh, and if they are clean they are not harmful and can even be useful. During the First World War they were bred for use in hospitals to clean up the wounds of soldiers with gangrene by eating the dead flesh. But some British greenbottles (flies similar to bluebottles) and some foreign bluebottles produce maggots that will attack living flesh. Such species often lay their eggs on sheep and the maggots make nasty open sores beneath the fleece that sometimes cause the death of the poor beast. This problem, commonly called 'fly-strike' by shepherds, can sometimes be very serious in Australia, South Africa and Britain. Other animals may be attacked in this way too.

After 2–21 days, depending on where they are, the maggots turn into pupae. Their outer skin hardens into a case and turns dark brown. Usually the pupae drop off the meat or body. In the olden days, every monastery had its carp pond – the monks enjoyed the delicious fish for meals on Fridays, the traditional day for eating fish. They would hang some dead rabbits over the pond, and bluebottle maggots would soon be feeding on the bodies. When the maggots turned into pupae and dropped off the meat, the fish were swimming below, ready to gobble them up. It was a sort of mediaeval automatic fish-feeding device!

Maggots and pupae of a bluebottle

Maggots are much used by fishermen as fish-bait. There are even maggot-farms where millions of maggots are bred each week from specially chosen bluebottles and feed on tons of waste fish. Such farms are very smelly and are usually right out in the country. Fishermen can buy live maggots that have been coloured with non-poisonous dyes. Every fisherman has his own idea of which colour is likely to appeal most to a particular kind of fish on a particular day.

After a period that may be as short as 3 days, though it is much longer in winter, the adult fly cracks its way out of the pupal case by puffing up a special bladder with blood. The new bluebottle is at first soft and flimsy with limp wings, but it immediately swallows air and puffs itself up inside to over twice the size. This pressure forces blood into the wings and stretches them. 20–30 minutes after emerging, the wings are ready to use, and within 1–2 hours the body-casing of the bluebottle has hardened and darkened.

It is a very good thing that flies that breed so quickly have so many enemies. Many other insects eat them, and so do a whole range of other creatures, including bats, cats and many smaller mammals. All these help to keep under control a creature that is a great pest, and one of the most unwelcome members of the zoo in the town.

The mediaeval monks' automatic carp-feeding device

Attracted by smell received via their antennae, flies find meat with great ease